Tom's Field Trip

Ryan Connolly

New York

Published in 2013 by The Rosen Publishing Group, Inc.
29 East 21st Street, New York, NY 10010

Copyright © 2013 by The Rosen Publishing Group, Inc.

All rights reserved. No part of this book may be reproduced in any form without permission in writing from the publisher, except by a reviewer.

Book Design: Michael Harmon

Photo Credits: Cover perrush/Shutterstock.com; p. 4 Darrin Henry/Shutterstock.com; p. 5 Morgan Lane Photography/Shutterstock.com; p. 6 PNC/Brand X Pictures/Getty Images; p. 7 Santje09/Shutterstock.com; p. 8 neelsky/Shutterstock.com; p. 9 tratong/Shutterstock.com; p. 10 (polar bears) Sean Gallup/Staff/Getty Images News/Getty Images; p. 10 (brown bear) ZSSD/Minden Pictures/Getty Images; p. 11 Kamira/Shutterstock.com; p. 12 Bobkeenan Photography/Shutterstock.com; p. 13 lipik/Shutterstock.com; p. 14 Image Source/the Agency Collection/Getty Images; p. 16 (bus driver) Kzenon/Shutterstock.com.

ISBN: 978-1-4488-8971-6
6-pack ISBN: 978-1-4488-8972-3

Manufactured in the United States of America

CPSIA Compliance Information: Batch #WS12RC: For further information contact Rosen Publishing, New York, New York at 1-800-237-9932.

Word Count: 141

Contents

A Class Trip	**4**
At the Zoo	**6**
Favorite Animals	**11**
Building Words	**15**
Words to Know	**16**
Index	**16**

This is Tom.

He has many friends in his class.

Today, Tom's class is going on a field trip.

They get on a big bus.

They meet a nice bus driver.

Tom's class is going to the zoo!
Many animals live at the zoo.

First, Tom sees a lion.

It's sleepy.

It's taking a nap.

Then, Tom sees a tiger.
It roars very loudly!

Tom's class sees many birds.
They're very colorful.

They see many bears, too.
The brown bears and polar bears are playful.

Tom's friend Jess likes the giraffes.

They're a lot taller than she is!

Tom's teacher likes the zebras.

Zebras are striped animals.

Their stripes are black and white.

Tom likes the elephants.

A mother elephant is much bigger than a baby elephant.

Have you ever been to a zoo?
What animals did you like the most?

Building Words

drive	→	drive**r**
sleep	→	sleep**y**
loud	→	loud**ly**
color	→	color**ful**
play	→	play**ful**
tall	→	tall**er**
teach	→	teach**er**
stripe	→	stripe**d**
big	→	big**ger**

Words to Know

bus driver

polar bears

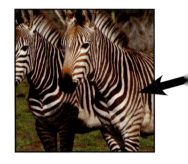
stripes

Index

bears, 10
birds, 9
elephants, 13
giraffes, 11
lion, 7

tiger, 8
zebras, 12
zoo, 6, 14